First edition for the United States and Canada published
in 2003 by Barron's Educational Series, Inc.

First edition for Great Britain published 2003 by Hodder
Wayland, an imprint of Hodder Children's Books

All inquiries should be addressed to:
Barron's Educational Series, Inc.
250 Wireless Boulevard
Hauppauge, NY 11788
http://www.barronseduc.com

Library of Congress Catalog Card No. 2002111583

EAN-13: 978-0-7641-2460-0
Date of Manufacture : December 2016
Manufactured by : Shenzhen Wing King Tong Paper Products Co. Ltd.,
Shenzhen, Guangdong, China.

Printed in China
19 18 17 16 15 14 13 12 11

Disclaimer
The web site addresses (URLs) included in this book were
valid at the time of going to press. However, because of
the nature of the Internet, it is possible that some addresses
may have changed, or sites may have changed or closed
down since publication. While the publisher regrets any
inconvenience this may cause readers, no responsibility for
any such changes will be accepted by the publisher.

I Can Be Safe

A FIRST LOOK AT SAFETY

PAT THOMAS
ILLUSTRATED BY LESLEY HARKER

BARRON'S

Everyone needs to be safe.
"Safe" means you are
not in any danger
of getting hurt.

Most of us have special places that make us feel safe and special people we trust.

There are lots of people who care about you and want to help you understand the difference between what is safe and what is not.

Your parents, teachers, and other adults in your
community all want to help you learn all you
can about being safe so that you can
grow up healthy and strong.

You probably already know lots of different ways to keep yourself safe. Maybe you wear special clothing when you play sports.

You may stop, look, and listen before crossing a road. Or maybe you know to hold on to someone's hand in crowded places.

What about you?

What other things can you do to stay safe?
At home? At school?
In the playground? On the street?

There are other things you should know as well. You should know your name, your parents' names, and your phone number.

That way, if you ever get lost you can get someone to help you find your family again.

555-1234
4 STAR PLACE
ANY TOWN
MR. JOHN JONES
MRS. MARY JONES

You should also know how to dial the emergency number (911) in case of an accident.

What about you?

Do you know this important information about yourself? Have you talked with your parents about what to do in emergencies? What have they said?

Did you know that each of us also has a special feeling that lets us know when things are not safe? This feeling is called fear, an instinct that helps warn us when something is wrong or we are in danger.

When you feel unsafe, fear can make your tummy or your head feel funny. It can make your heart beat faster and make it hard to breathe. Always trust your feelings – they are there to protect you.

Sometimes it can be fun
to feel scared. It can
feel exciting.

Especially if you know
there is no real danger.

17

But sometimes you feel scared for a good reason, such as when someone you do not trust tries to talk to you or touch you in a way that causes you to feel unsafe or afraid.

This does not happen very often, but when it does you should know that it is OK to be rude to this person, to say no, and even to shout at them and kick them if you need to.

Your body belongs to you and you have a right to protect it. A good rule to remember is that people – especially those you don't feel comfortable with – should never touch any part of your body that is covered by your swimsuit.

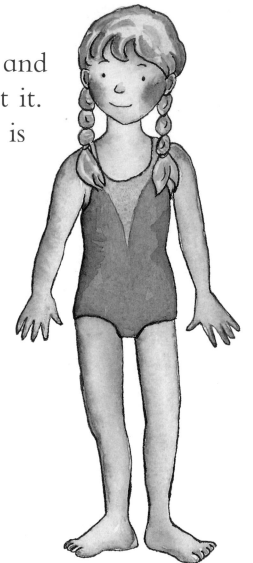

If this happens you should tell a parent or trusted grown-up. They can make sure it does not happen again.

What about you?

Can you think of some other ways to stay safe if a stranger, or even someone you know but do not trust, gets too close to you? What do your parents say you should do?

Sometimes in order to be safe you have
to learn a new skill or a new set of rules.

And sometimes you have to learn to say no to things that look fun but your fear warns you could be dangerous.

Everyone forgets to act safely once in a while. We have all gotten lost or scared or hurt at some time in our lives.

The important thing is to learn
from mistakes and be more
careful next time.

KEEP
OUT

A big part of growing
up is learning to look after
yourself in lots of different
situations. When you feel safe you
do not have to worry about anything
or anyone hurting you.

You can relax and
enjoy yourself wherever you
are, whoever you are with, and
whatever you are doing.

27

HOW TO USE THIS BOOK

Keeping children safe is everyone's responsibility. Schools do an enormous amount of work in this area by providing lessons, talks, and film and video presentations on many aspects of personal safety. Visits from police officers, firefighters, and others who are willing to talk about safety issues have become the norm. However, lessons in safety must be continually reinforced by parents.

Consider some of the following suggestions for keeping your child safe in any situation.

First of all, keep your perspective. The majority of children do reach adulthood safe and well. Abductions and abuse, while devastating, are still rare.

Most parents provide day-to-day safety instructions without even thinking: "Don't touch that; it's hot." "Hold my hand; it's crowded in here." "Look both ways before crossing the street." "Wash your hands before you eat." "Use your sunscreen."

Bigger issues require a little more effort. As early as possible, you should make a conscious effort to ensure that your children know their full name, their parents' full names, where they live, including the house number, street, city, and zip code, and their full telephone number. In addition, children should be given some instruction on dialing the emergency number (911) for help.

Keep a list of important phone numbers somewhere obvious – for instance, stuck to the refrigerator with a colorful magnet – so that children can make use of these in an emergency. Making this kind of list could also be a good homework project for young children.

Be patient. Learning to take care of yourself is an ongoing lesson. Small children cannot possibly be expected to think through every situation from a safety point of view before acting. That's a parent's job. Just keep reinforcing the message and giving them opportunities to talk about it. Issuing orders is rarely a good way to get children to think about safety. Instead, lead by example. Learn to talk about safety issues as and when the opportunity arises: "Did that boy look both ways before crossing the street?" "Should that little girl be swimming on her own?" Let your children think it through and come up with the answers themselves.

Schools might consider holding a safety fair each year. Representatives of the police and fire departments, ambulance service, local sports and recreation facilities, and local council could be invited to put up displays and give talks and demonstrations. Follow up with classwork about what the children learned on that day.

You can talk to children about anything if you do it in a matter-of-fact way. Abuse and abduction, for example, can and should be talked about from an early age – just make sure the information you give is appropriate to your child's age and understanding of the world. Think through what you would like to say before you say it.

Reinforce the idea that a child's body is personal property and that no one has the right to touch or hurt it. When discussing the topic of body privacy, try to use real words such as "penis" and "vagina." Let your children know that they must tell you if anyone ever talks or teases them about their body or tries to touch them in a way that feels wrong. Stress the fact that they should never keep any secrets from you about this subject, no matter what anyone tells them!

For a whole variety of reasons, children may be left at home alone for varying lengths of time. Children need to understand that they must never let anyone know they are home alone. Nor should they answer the door when home alone unless a visitor is expected (and always check who is there before opening the door). If someone calls on the phone and asks to speak to an adult, children at home alone should say that their parents are busy at the moment, take a message, then politely hang up. Children should never give out any personal information (name, phone number, address, and so on) over the telephone or Internet.

To avoid a situation where a stranger tricks a child into coming with them, some families have a secret password that only the adults and children know. This password should be used only in an extreme emergency situation, such as if a neighbor or someone the child doesn't know has to unexpectedly pick up or take care of your child. Once the password is used, you need to change to a new password!

GLOSSARY

instinct knowing something without being told. Your instinct is like your personal radar or X-ray vision. It helps you to see invisible clues that help you judge when something is right or not.

stranger someone you don't know. The most dangerous strangers are people you don't know who try to act like your friend, or those who act one way in front of adults but a different way when they are alone with you.

FURTHER READING

The Safety Book for Active Kids
by Linda Schwartz (Learning Works, 1995)

Keeping Kids Safe
by K. L. Wheatley (Leading Edge Publishing, 1998)

It's MY Body
by Lori Freeman (Parenting Press, 1984)

The Berenstain Bears Learn About Strangers
by Stan Berenstain, Jan Berenstain
(Random House, 1985)

RESOURCES

Child Safety and Health Resource Guide
http://pasture.ecn.purdue.edu/~agsafety/risk/Resource/TOC.html

Provides lists of organizations by region, by state, and by topic, such as poison control, rural health and safety, fire prevention, and so on.

National SAFE KIDS Campaign
111 Michigan Avenue, N.W.
Washington, D.C. 20010-2970
(202)884-4993 Fax: (301)650-8038

National Safety Council (NSC)
1-800-621-7619

A nongovernmental public service organization committed to significantly reducing human suffering and economic losses arising from preventable causes.

American Academy of Pediatrics (AAP)
1-800-433-9016

Provides information on pediatric care and safety.